Interfaith Workbook for Children: for parents and teachers too

By Michael R. Basso

I0417554

About the Author

Dr. Michael R. Basso has been the author and coauthor of several children's books which are focused upon teaching children, parents and educators about people with disabilities.

Michael has significant experience as college level educator in psychology at Yale University and the University of Connecticut and well as being a leader in quality and reliability engineering and management in industry. His experience also includes being a consultant, researcher, and newspaper columnist. Michael is the president of the Connecticut Holistic Health Association.

Dr. Basso has a Ph.D. in professional psychology and biomedical systems, an MS in engineering science, and an MBA with a focus in executive leadership and an interdisciplinary Professional Development Diploma in pathophysiology, neural systems, and education. He also holds a BS in electrical engineering. Michael is certified in quality and reliability engineering and quality auditing, as well as a variety of health related areas.

Preface – for parents and teachers

Spirituality means many things to many people. However, there are some core themes that are very common. For instance, a sense of hope, the drive of inspiration, ethics and charity can be found within many religions as well as within those who are spiritual, yet choose to follow their own path. Some folks even choose to take bits and pieces from many religions and follow none exclusively.

The purpose of this little workbook is to teach children early on about common themes and differences. By focusing on facts and interesting points, the cognitive, or thinking, path towards persuasion against prejudice can be better used to facilitate tolerance.

This book will be told as a story so that the important concepts may best better personalized.

Each section will have a section for the author's reflections about a particular religion which will be followed by an opportunity for the child to add their own reflections (and/or those of their, parents, teachers of others)

Topics Covered

Before there were Religions

Some Common Religions (Alphabetical order)

> Buddhist
>
> Christian
>
>> Baptist
>>
>> Catholic
>>
>> Protestant
>
> Hindu
>
> Islam
>
>> Sufi
>
> Hebrew
>
>> Kabala
>
> Sikhism
>
> Zoroastrianism

Modern Religions

"Hi, Mama, I had this real cool dream last night. Jesus came to me and talked to me. He said that he loves all religions and that each one has a purpose. Then there was a campfire and children from many faiths were sitting around it."

that

"Wow, Sammy is cool!"

"And then, Mama, Jesus said that there is a connection between all religions & that some kids believe in God in other ways besides religion. Jesus even said to me that people believed in God long before he or even Moses walked this Earth."

"Is that true, mama?"

"You bet, Sammy, the Native Americans had ways to worship the creator (God) and its creation (the universe) long before there were religions or books like we have today."

you called someone called – what's

"Mama, God 'it' and at school God a woman up with that? I thought God was a man."

"Well, son, everybody has their own beliefs and nobody can change what someone else really thinks. Many people think that God is neither man nor woman and choose to call God, it."

"Ok, mama, I understand. Some kids think that God is somehow a light or a sound or both even! How cool is that, mama? That's what some kids in school think."

"Son, when I was a boy, some people I knew even believed that we come back many times. We know from science that the cells in our bodies are spread from generation to generation – lots of people believe that our spirits take on new bodies. That's called reincarnation. Some of my friends even believed that we can come back as an animal. That's called transmigration."

"Wow, dad, that's awesome. Some kids in school believe that each time we die or be reborn that our cells remember and so do our spirits. They say in their religion that they can even remember what happened and as they remember and in other ways are reminded of all that pain that we become stronger and even more capable."

"Wow, Sammy, I never thought of that stuff, but it makes sense to me as a scientist. Makes me think that somehow all that pain and death somehow made turtles develop hard shells and polar bears develop that thick fur...hmmmmm!"

"Daddy, the dream went on and on like it was happening all night!"

"Tell me more, son. I had a dream like that when I was a kid, but I was afraid to tell my parents – because they said that their religion was the only way and I didn't want them to get mad at me."

"I understand, Dad. Lots of people fight over religion. I don't know what God wants, but I think that God wants us to get along with people from other faiths."

"I agree with you, son."

"Mama, next thing the campfire got real big and

10

turned all lots of colors, including a beautiful blue color that I really liked."

"Then King came to dream. He awesome – he he didn't want

Reverend me in the was said that people to

fight over things that he said, but he wanted people from all religions and all colors to get along."

"Mama it was real cool when he showed me an old time singer, called Elvis, singing beautiful Negro spirituals, like in our Baptist church."

11

"The music was real beautiful, Mama, and Reverend King said that he was so proud of Elvis and that he loved his spiritual gospel music too."

"Then he told me about the purpose of Baptism and why the Baptist church came about."

"Mama, I remember when my friend, Billy's mama died hundreds of people came visit the family and they some much loved the beautiful music and how kind every one was."

"Dr. King said that that it was not Ok for blacks to be prejudice either and that it was great to learn about all religions."

"I know it was only a dream, but it was sooo real, mama."

"Next in the dream, my friend Sarah came to me _ she's Jewish."

"In the dream, there were two stones and they contained the Ten Commandments like in our Bible, mama."

"How neat, son."

"The man that was with Sarah had a little hat on his head and there was a woman too. They were both some kind of minister."

"They are called Rabbis in the Jewish faith and that a little hat is called a **yarmulke** (pronounced *yah ma ka*)."

"The man in the dream said to Sarah and I that it was Jewish law for a man to wear a yarmulke when praying."

"The Jewish holy book, called the Talmud, states that men cover their heads…." The Rabbi also said that it helps people to know that a person is Jewish."

"Wow that was some dream, Sammy."

"You bet, dad."

"Son, some also study the Cabbala."

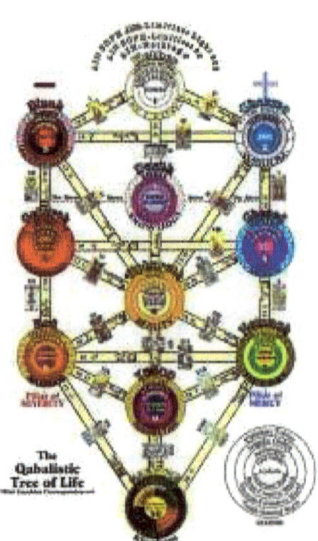

Jewish people

"They describe something called the tree of life – they talk about beauty, joy and even angels and other beings that are said to help humans and all life and how all these things work together."

"Then a beautiful angel came to us in the dream – it said that angels can take any form, but for my sake, it had beautiful wings, like we saw on TV."

"The angel took me to the Vatican in Rome, where I saw the Pope giving mass. It was beautiful, mama. All these priests dressed in red and the smell of some kind of incense."

"Those priests are called Cardinals, Sam," his dad explained. The Catholic Church is very big, so they have different levels – Cardinals work directly for the Pope. Then they have Bishops at the next level and Priests after that. They have brothers who are working to be priests and nuns who are not priests – they are ladies who are working to help the church and the community. The incense was called frankincense."

"Then the pope gave out a little bread thing some of the people attending mass."

"In the dream, a very special nun came to us and told us that there are other Christian churches and that they are called Protestant. She

18

also said that the little bread was called a host and that it is also called the Holy Eucharist and that that part of the mass is called communion."

"Just then, a real cool Native American came into the dream with an awesome head dress….and then I saw a tribe dancing around a fire and a medicine woman shaking some kind of rattle. And then some people from Africa were there too and they were beating some real cool drums – I could feel the beat in my dreams. "

19

"Then the nun said that there are lots of Christian religions, including the Lutheran, Presbyterian, Episcopal and more.

"The Lutherans, started by Martin Luther in 1517, didn't like some of the fancy rituals that the Catholics did. They believe that only faith in Jesus was necessary and that God can be nice to someone without all the fancy stuff. They called the niceness grace."

"The Episcopal church started right after the revolutionary war. They use a special book called the *Book of Common Prayer*. The Episcopal spent a lot of time teaching black people about the church."

"Presbyterianism started in Scotland in 1557 by Jon Hicks and they are run by elders. Ministers can be teaching elders and others from the church may be ruling elders."

"Well son, the Jehovah Witnesses and the Mormon who walk around the neighborhood are also Christians."

"Mama, a kid in school said that his family were Jehovah Witnesses and they believe in Jesus too, but they don't celebrate Christmas – huh, I'm confused."

"Hamm. Well they believe that the bible teaches only to celebrate Christ's death at Passover time. "

"Son, the Mormons are very strict about dressing in ways that are modest – so they have to wear a special undergarment to remind them about that. They also don't allow coffee, tea, alcohol and tobacco as a way to be healthy. The religion was started by Joseph Smith, Jr. after he found some special writing buried in upstate New York – he claimed that an angel guided him. "

"Thanks, dad."

"What about those Hari Krishna people we saw at the airport a few years ago, dad? Are they Christians too?"

"No, son. They are Hindus. They believe that Krishna was like Jesus in a way. They sing a chant that goes like this – sometimes for hours

Hari Krishna, Hari Krishna, Krishna, Krishna, Rama, Rama."

"As a scientist I study meditation and music and wow those chants really do relax people and make them feel better. And their vegetarian foods are delicious."

"That's neat dad. I want to be a scientist too some day and study that cool stuff."

"You can be son. Your mama studied lots about religion when she was in college and when she went to divinity school."

"Sammy, I also learned that the Hindu believes in lots of Gods and Deities that are said the rule nature – like angels in a way."

"They also have lots of other chants, including one called –

'Om Nama Shivia'

"That reminds me of the

Kirtan

people who came to play music and sing at my school. They said that they were taking ancient Hindu chants and playing and singing them in an American way. It was so cool and the music was so cool. They even added some Hebrew (Jewish) stuff and Gospel music and stuff about Jesus. They called it

Omni

They said, like Reverend King - that all religions are important and all have their purpose."

26

"Mama there was also a kid at school who was Buddhist. She did some kind of chant too and the teacher made us learn it for a history class. The Buddhist chant was called

'Om Mani Padme Hum'

They chant on Chang's one even put the prayer flags. dad even had hanging from the mirror in their car."

27

They said that some people do these chants for hours and hours every say. Some pray with a prayer wheel."

"Chang's dad also said that they read many books and that there are many types of Buddhism. He believes in a book called the

Tibetan book of the Dead."

"Yikes, Sammy."

"No, it's not scary, dad. Chang said that some Buddhists even talk to people after they die and that what people believe has lots to do with what happens after they die and even who they meet - or think they meet - right after they die."

"Wow, we should study that. religions are a lot Some even believe hear when our our mommy's when we are born in some way. Real

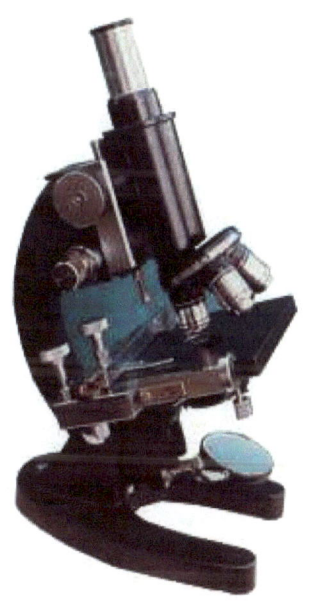

scientists Some like science. that what he bodies are in tummy or can affect us science in a

way."

"Sammy, your sister, Matilda, used to chant in her Yoga class. She would chant

Om

All the time."

"Sammy, one night she had a dream and in the dream she heard lots of different kinds of music – like bagpipes, harps, flutes and more."

"Mommy, once I had a dream that a whole orchestra was playing - and I had the same dream for weeks."

"Wow, I had a dream once where there was just different colors. And then a voice somehow said to me that this was one of the many heavens."

"That's cool too. That's funny – same thing happened in my dream about music. Hmmmm."

"There is a fellow that I work with that practices the religion called

Islam

He reads from a book called the Koran and he prays six  times every day."

"Wow, he must love his religion."

"He sure does, Sammy – he's a very nice man. His family even does some kind of fast once a year that lasts for a whole month – called Ramadan."

"Awesome!"

"Mama what are Sufis?"

"Well Sufis are part people who Cabbala are – the Jewish  Sammy, the of Islam, like the study the part of Judaism religion."

33

"I saw a kid spinning around in school at an assembly - and they said that he was a

Sufi

"Those are called Whirling Dervishes."

"Thanks, mama."

"You're welcome, son."

"Sammy, the Sufi's also chant like the some of the other religions – one of their chants is called

HOO."

"That reminds me of that cool old man who used to meditate for hours and hours down in the forest. He was so kind and nice and had the coolest Turban and a long white beard."

"He would sometimes chant too and sometimes he would chant something like that – he called it the

HU"

"Sammy – we can find the HU and the Om also called AUM) in parts of many religions."

"Boys, the Sikh religion was started by Guru Nanak. There were 10 successive gurus who were the leaders of the religion. The last of the 10 was considered to be a HOLY BOOK called Guru Granth Sahib Ji."

"What!"

"Yes, they felt that their teaching got better and better and so the book was a great way for people to follow. They chant the holy names of

36

God – including **Ek omkar.** The Sikhs often sing holy names and practice Kirtan – using singing and using instruments to recite holy verses."

"Mama, what is Zoroasterism?

A new kid in school is part of that religion _ I never heard of it."

"It's a very old Persian religion. Their holy book is the

Avesta

That book includes five sacred hymns, called Ganthas. They believe that there is a constant battle between good and evil such as lies and truth. They may be the first religion that believed in one God – whom they called Ahura Mazda."

"Wow that is real cool, mama. Dr. King meant what he said. There are so many religions and they all should get along."

"In one of my dreams I just heard a humming sound - almost like the Huuuuuuu sound dragged out and in another one I heard an OM sound."

OM

"Well, Sammy maybe there is something very special about the word of God that is mentioned in so many religions."

"Go figure, mama."

"Yes son, go figure."

"Remember, son I have friends that are Unitarian-Universalists, Members of the Society for Ethical Culture, Spiritualists, Eckists, Scientologists, Theosophists, Self-realization fellowship members, and several more….Please think of some of the MODERN religions that we haven't talked about YET! There may be some ideas that you believe and other ideas that you do not. Most important of all, please be tolerant of others regardless of what you may believe. That's OK. Let's talk about them ALL as a family. Maybe we will learn some things that we had not thought of."

Workbook Section

Feel free to ask your parents or others to help here

 Please name five religions that are Christian

1)

2)

3)

4)

5)

 What are some things that are special about ISLAM?

1)

2)

3)

4)

5)

What are some things that are different about the Jewish religion?

1)

2)

3)

4)

5)

 What is the Hindu religion all about?

1)

2)

3)

4)

5)

 How can all religions collaborate and cooperate?

1)

2)

3)

4)

5)

 What are some general ideas that fit your idea of a religion?

1)

2)

3)

4)

5)

6)

7)

Notes

www.ingramcontent.com/pod-product-compliance
Lightning Source LLC
Chambersburg PA
CBHW041515280526
45792CB00004B/1258